Early Congresses

Wendy Conklin, M. A.

Table of Contents

Paving the Way 3

A Taste of Freedom 4–5

Taxation Without Representation 6–7

Bringing the Colonies Together 8–9

The First Continental Congress 10–11

One Last Chance 12–13

Independence or Not? 14–15

The Declaration of Independence 16–17

Congress Chooses a Commander in Chief 18–19

Articles of Confederation 20–21

Constitutional Convention .22–23

Glossary 24

Index 25

Paving the Way

Before America was a country, no one dared to think that common people could make their own laws. Kings, queens, and priests were the only ones fit to govern. Or so they thought! A group of spirited men changed that way of thinking. They formed the first congresses in the colonies and led the way to freedom.

▲ Leaders of the Continental Congress: John Adams, Gouverneur Morris, Alexander Hamilton, and Thomas Jefferson

A Taste of Freedom

Andrew Hamilton, a famous lawyer, made history in 1735. He was the lawyer for a man named Peter Zenger. Zenger had spoken out against the governor, Mr. William Cosby. Back then, no one spoke out against the colonial rulers.

This governor was under the rule of the British king. Everyone knew he was a rotten governor. He had the elections fixed so that certain people won. He also took money and land from the colonists. Zenger printed these accusations (ak-yoo-ZAY-shuhnz) in his New York newspaper. These accusations made the governor angry. So, the governor accused Zenger of lying about him and printing lies.

The Hamilton Name

Don't get Andrew Hamilton and Alexander Hamilton mixed up! Alexander Hamilton was also a lawyer. Later, he became the first secretary to the treasury of the United States.

Andrew Hamilton

Common people made up the jury at Zenger's trial. Hamilton believed the jury was smart enough to decide Zenger's guilt or innocence. He told this to the jury, and they decided that Zenger was not guilty. The British governor was very upset. For the first time, the colonists began to see that they could govern themselves.

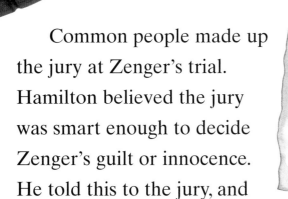

Learning from the Iroquois

The American Indians gave the colonial leaders some great ideas. The Iroquois (EAR-uh-kwoy) tribe had six nations that ruled themselves. They worked together in times of war or for business.

▼ Courtroom scene of a jury trial in the 1700s

Taxation Without Representation

Way back in 1215, Great Britain had a power-hungry ruler named King John. "I can do anything I want!" he thought. The British were tired of being his servants, so they rebelled and took over the capital city of London. Then, they made King John sign an agreement called the Magna Carta. This agreement granted rights to the British people through Parliament (PAR-luh-muhnt). Parliament is the British **legislative** (LEJ-is-lay-tiv) **branch** that represents its people and makes its laws.

▼ **King John signs the Magna Carta**

Through Parliament, British people voted on their laws and taxes. The colonists thought of themselves as British **citizens** (SIT-uh-zuhns). But there was no one to represent the colonists in the British Parliament. The colonists called this "taxation without representation."

When Englishmen went to the New World, they took copies of the Magna Carta with them. Every time Parliament approved new taxes without their vote, the colonists felt cheated. They vowed to fight with a sword in one hand and the Magna Carta in the other.

Franklin in England

Ben Franklin worked to show England how the colonists felt. The colonists did not know how much he stood up for them. Some colonists even threatened his home in Pennsylvania for a while because they thought he was a traitor.

▼ British House of Parliament in 1608

Benjamin Franklin

Bringing the Colonies Together

It was clear to the colonists that they did not have the same rights as people living in England. Because of this, they stopped thinking of themselves as British colonists. Colonists began calling themselves names such as Virginians, North Carolinians, and New Englanders.

Samuel Adams had grown up in the colonies. He knew the colonies needed to break away from Great Britain. To do this, he had to get people angry with British rulers.

▼ **Samuel Adams**

Virginia's House of Burgesses

Virginia formed the first legislature elected by the people in the New World. It was called the House of Burgesses (BURR-juhs-uhs) and first met in this Jamestown church on July 30, 1619.

Adams wanted to find a way to bring the colonies together. He organized a group of colonists and called them the **Committees of Correspondence** (kor-uh-SPON-duhntz). Important leaders from different colonies made up these committees. They wrote letters to each other about problems and tried to offer help.

Adams also started a group called the Sons of Liberty. These men met secretly and made plans for how to make sure colonists had fair rights. It was through these groups that Adams motivated others to think about freedom.

Common Sense

Thomas Paine wrote a booklet called *Common Sense*. This booklet told the colonists that they could live without a king. This was a **radical** idea at that time.

Thomas Paine

▼ Newspaper advertisement for the Sons of Liberty

ADVERTISEMENT.

THE Members of the Affociation of the Sons of Liberty, are requefted to meet at the City-Hall, at one o'Clock, To-morrow, (being Friday) on Bufi-nefs of the utmoft Importance;—And every other Friend to the Liberties, and Trade of America, are hereby moft cordially invited, to meet at the fame Time and Place. *The Committee of the Affociation.*

Thurfday, NEW-YORK, 16th December, 1773.

COMMON SENSE;

ADDRESSED TO THE

INHABITANTS

OF

AMERICA,

On the following interefting

SUBJECTS.

I. Of the Origin and Defign of Government in general, with concife Remarks on the Englifh Conftitution.

II. Of Monarchy and Hereditary Succeffion.

III. Thoughts on the prefent State of American Affairs.

IV. Of the prefent Ability of America, with fome mi cellaneous Reflections.

Man knows no Mafter fave crea ing HEAVEN, Or thofe whom choice and common good ordain

The First Continental Congress

Samuel Adams wanted to separate from Great Britain. He knew the colonists could be trusted to rule themselves. The members of the Committees of Correspondence met in Philadelphia in 1774. These leaders formed the First **Continental** (kon-tuh-NEN-tuhl) **Congress**.

Knowing that Great Britain could accuse them of **treason**, they kept their meetings a secret. Some of the **delegates** thought they should try to work with Great Britain. Others thought it was best to break away and declare war.

Georgia's Absence

The delegates came from every colony except Georgia. The British governor of Georgia prevented delegates from going to the meeting.

Three delegates on ▶ their way to the First Continental Congress

Congress urged the colonists to stop buying British goods. They also ordered the colonies to form **militias** (muh-LISH-uhs). Most importantly, they wrote a letter called the Declaration of Rights and Grievances to the king. This letter explained how they felt about taxes and their lack of rights. It was a respectful letter. The delegates hoped that the king would have Parliament change the laws. The delegates agreed to meet seven months later to hear the king's response.

Patrick Henry's Influence

Patrick Henry was a delegate who encouraged others to think as one group. He said, "The distinctions between Virginia, New York, and New England are no more. I am not a Virginian, but an American."

Patrick Henry

▼ Declaration of Rights and Grievances (GREE-vuhn-zez)

▲ Session of the Continental Congress

John Hancock was elected president of the Second Continental Congress.

One Last Chance

The king ignored the letter from the Continental Congress. British Parliament passed a law making it illegal for the colonies to trade with each other. Now, the colonies would have to buy British products to survive. Any delegates who had been loyal to the king before changed their minds at this point.

The Second Continental Congress met as planned, and they had big decisions to make. Each delegate was expected to share his opinion about the situation. This took quite a long time because there were many delegates.

Declaring independence from Great Britain was a big step. There were still some who wanted to give the king one last chance to avoid war. They wrote a letter called the **Olive Branch Petition** (puh-TISH-uhn). This letter asked the king to repeal the tax laws. It also promised that the protests would stop if he met their demands. Once again the king chose to ignore their requests.

The Responsibilities of Congress

Congress began printing money and creating an army.

▲ **British Parliament buildings in London**

Independence or Not?

For months and months the delegates debated. "Should we declare independence from Great Britain?" they asked.

For many it was hard to imagine life without a king. They wondered how they would get a post office up and running. How they would pay the bills in this new country? How would the courts be run?

Others believed the only way to live was apart from Great Britain. Patrick Henry from Virginia was a gifted public speaker. He gave a famous speech saying, "I know not what course others may take, but as for me, give me liberty or give me death."

▲ Patrick Henry addressing the Virginia House of Burgesses

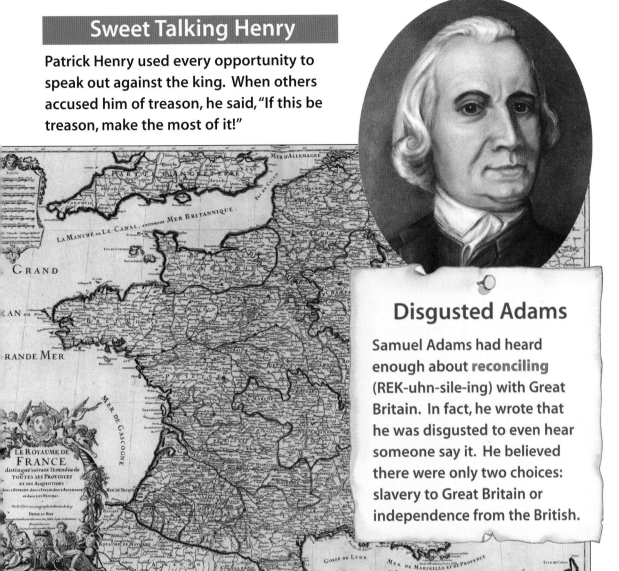

Sweet Talking Henry

Patrick Henry used every opportunity to speak out against the king. When others accused him of treason, he said, "If this be treason, make the most of it!"

Disgusted Adams

Samuel Adams had heard enough about **reconciling** (REK-uhn-sile-ing) with Great Britain. In fact, he wrote that he was disgusted to even hear someone say it. He believed there were only two choices: slavery to Great Britain or independence from the British.

▲ This map shows France, a country that helped the colonies in the Revolution

Congress knew they had to make **alliances** (uh-LIE-uhn-suhz) with foreign countries. The colonists would surely need France's help to defeat the British. It was up to Congress to convince France to help the colonies win the war.

The Declaration of Independence

A committee was formed to write the Declaration of Independence. The main author was a quiet Virginian named Thomas Jefferson. The **document** states that the king had wronged the colonies. It describes a good government. Then, it tells the world why the colonists no longer belong to Great Britain.

Benjamin Franklin and John Adams reviewing
▼ Thomas Jefferson's draft of the Declaration of Independence

On June 28, 1776, a draft of the document was shared with Congress. The delegates debated the document for a few days. On July 2, it was time to vote. It was up to the delegates from each colony to cast their votes. Twelve of the thirteen colonies voted for the declaration. New York had to wait to hear back from leaders in their state.

The King's Diary

On July 4, 1776, King George III wrote in his diary, "Nothing of importance happened today."

Finally, on July 4, 1776, Congress formally approved the Declaration of Independence. The men knew that signing the document meant that they were traitors against England. They understood that they were signing their own death warrants if the war was lost.

Resolution from July 2, 1776, in which the Continental Congress agrees to independence from England

Slavery in the Declaration

Jefferson had included an anti-slavery section in his early drafts of the document. Some colonial delegates refused to sign it. To keep the colonies from splitting, Congress agreed to remove that section.

Congress Chooses a Commander in Chief

With the militia ready to fight, the colonists needed a leader. At the Second Continental Congress, John Adams stood up to speak. John was Samuel Adams's cousin, and he was just as smart. He told the Congress what everyone had been thinking. They needed both an army and a general. Adams said, "I know just the man for the job!"

▼ Washington being nominated as commander in chief by the Continental Congress

John Adams was a close friend to John Hancock. Since Hancock had once been a soldier, he thought that he was the likely choice to be general.

Adams described the man he had in mind. To everyone's surprise the description did not fit Hancock. Instead, Adams **nominated** George Washington to be the general.

Of course, Hancock was disappointed, but he knew Washington was a good choice. He quickly wrote the order that named Washington the commander of the Continental Army.

Hiring Washington

George Washington took the job of general on one condition. He would not accept money for this job.

George Washington

▼ **Washington's commission as commander in chief**

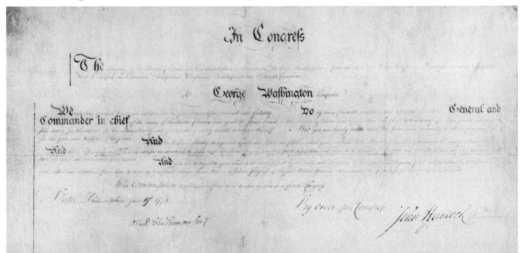

In Congress

George Washington

We, Commander in chief

General and

Articles of Confederation

Congress knew they had to hurry and set up some form of government. A strong central government was out of the question. They had had enough of the British **monarchy** (MON-uhr-kee). Congress wanted to set up a government with limited powers.

In November 1777, Congress wrote the Articles of Confederation (kuhn-fed-uh-RAY-shuhn). Once they were **ratified** in March 1781, these articles served as the first **constitution** of the United States. Unfortunately, this document did not give much power to anyone.

▼ **The Articles of Confederation**

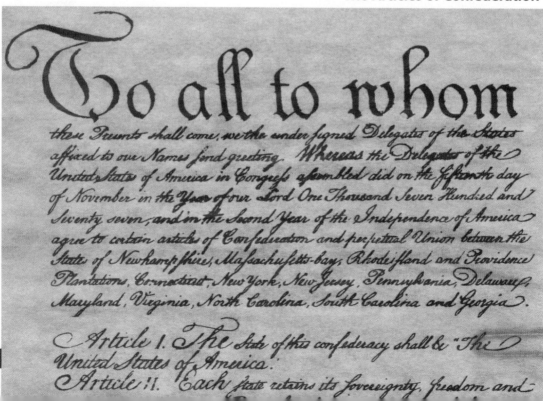

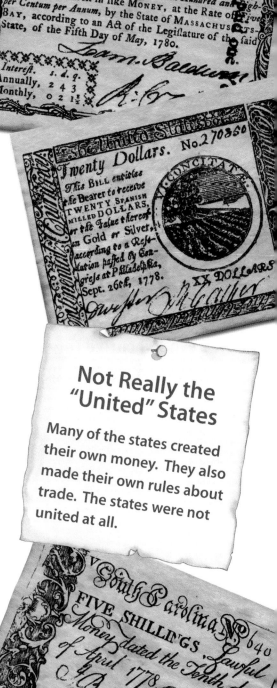

The small states were afraid they would not be represented. So the articles gave each state the same number of votes in Congress. This angered the large states, because they had more people. "Shouldn't we have more votes?" they argued.

Congress was busy making laws, enforcing laws, and punishing the criminals. It was just too much, and it was not working. The states did whatever they wanted because the federal laws were not enforced.

Not Really the "United" States

Many of the states created their own money. They also made their own rules about trade. The states were not united at all.

Constitutional Convention

After seeing that the Articles of Confederation weren't working, a **Constitutional** (kon-stuh-TOO-shuhn-uhl) **Convention** was held. These men wrote a new Constitution. They set up three branches of government that shared power: a congress, a president, and a court system.

This Constitution divided Congress into two parts: the House of Representatives (rep-ri-ZEN-tuh-tivz) and the Senate. The number of representatives in the House is determined by each state's population. Every state elects only two representatives to the Senate. This is the legislative branch of the government. It makes the laws for the country.

An **executive** (eg-ZEK-yoo-tiv) **branch**, led by the president, was also organized. This branch makes sure the laws are followed.

▼ Signing of the U.S. Constitution

Independence Hall in Philadelphia, the meeting place of the Constitutional Convention

The Great Compromise

During the Constitutional Convention, people argued about how many representatives each state should have in Congress. People from the large states wanted to have many representatives because their states were big. People from the small states thought every state should have the same number of representatives. The two sides compromised and formed the House and the Senate.

The **judicial** (joo-DISH-uhl) **branch** is made up of the courts and judges. This branch of the government has to decide what the laws mean.

The country we enjoy today would not have been possible without the men from the first congresses. Their bravery and brilliance together helped form the United States.

Secretive Meeting

What went on in the Constitutional Convention was kept secret. The doors were locked and the windows were kept shut. The delegates felt that they could get more done without interruptions. Thankfully, James Madison kept notes about what happened and what was said.

Glossary

alliances—agreements with other countries

citizens—people who are members of a country and receive protection from it in return

Committees of Correspondence—a group of leaders from all over the colonies who wrote letters to each other asking for advice and support

constitution—document that outlines the laws that govern a country

Constitutional Convention—a meeting where delegates created and voted on the laws that would govern the United States

Continental Congress—meeting of delegates from the colonies to decide how to deal with Great Britain

delegates—people sent to represent and speak for a group

document—official government paper

executive branch—part of the government that must carry out the laws

judicial branch—part of the government that must decide what the laws mean

legislative branch—part of the government that makes the laws

militias—armies made up of men from the colonies

monarchy—rule of a country by a king or queen

nominated—suggested that a specific person to serve in a position or job

Olive Branch Petition—a letter to King George asking him to work with the colonists to prevent war; the olive branch is a symbol of peace

radical—a belief that is drastic, extreme, new, or groundbreaking

ratified—accepted through voting

reconciling—to return to harmony or friendship

treason—betraying one's country